MUFFINS

Scones, pikelets and waffles, too!

Shirley Bradstock

David Bateman

ACKNOWLEDGEMENTS

Thanks to all my friends who helped with recipes, in particular Linda, Rhona and Betsy; Barbara for her help at an awkward moment, and to my husband Mike for his encouragement.

For Rachel and Isabel

First published in 1991 by David Bateman Ltd
'Golden Heights', 32–34 View Road, Glenfield, Auckland, New Zealand

Copyright © 1991 Shirley G. Bradstock
Copyright © 1991 David Bateman Ltd

Reprinted 1992

ISBN 1 86953 072 1

Photography by John Daley
Typeset by Egan-Reid Ltd
Printed by Colorcraft

Jacket design by Errol McLeary

Cover: The classic blueberry muffin (p. 17).

Contents

MUFFINS

SCONES

PIKELETS

WAFFLES

ABBREVIATIONS AND CONVERSIONS

t	teaspoon	1 t	5 ml
T	tablespoon	1 T	20 ml
c	cup	1 c	250 ml
C	Celsius	1 cup flour	155 g
ml	millilitre	1 cup sugar	250 g
kg	kilogram	1 cup butter or margarine	250 g
cm	centimetre		
g	gram		
l	litre		
min.	minutes		

MMM...Muffins!

Introduction

Have I got some great muffin recipes for you! The main idea in writing this collection was to get together all those wonderful muffin recipes I'd tasted, seen or heard of over the years. Also, I wanted to present a book with recipes you could whip together in under 30 minutes. Most of us have one or two muffin recipes which are quick and dependably delicious, so it is refreshing (and reassuring) to have a whole book full of different, fast and reliable recipes you can turn to.

Very few of these muffin recipes are truly original. It is difficult to vary a basic muffin recipe too far and still have a muffin. I've had lots of help from friends all over the world who sent me their latest favourite muffin recipe, and I've spent many enjoyable hours in the kitchen concocting my version of some lovely muffin I might have tasted at a morning tea. It's been fun and I hope you will enjoy the exciting collection that has come out of it all.

Muffins are quick to make, so you can serve them fresh from the oven — in fact, that's the best way to have them. Lots of books, and people for that matter, have told me that muffins freeze nicely. I don't agree. Either you make the muffins fresh shortly before you need them (and that is easy because they don't take long) or don't bother. I think one of the joys of muffins is the moist, warm, delicate flavour you get from a freshly made muffin, not the reheated, chewy result from a frozen batch.

You can make up a muffin recipe and keep it in the refrigerator for weeks, pouring the batter into waiting muffin tins to be cooked whenever you want some. I personally think that is a little strange, kind of defeats part of the purpose of having fresh and different muffins, but I have friends who use that method often and quite successfully.

Quite a few of the recipes you'll be able to make with ingredients you usually have on hand in the kitchen. However, as you will notice upon glancing through the book, there are several rather special and different muffin recipes for which you will probably need to plan ahead. Let me assure you that they are indeed worth the trouble! You might try to trade half a cup of curacao with someone who has half a cup of frangelico so you don't have to buy such a lot of the more expensive ingredients, but then again, it is rather nice to have a small bottle on hand to have after dinner when guests are around.

Hints for baking good muffins

● Don't overmix the muffin batter. If you do, the muffins will not be as light as they should be. Overmixing breaks the elastic gluten in the flour and is one reason for tough muffins.

● Pre-heat your oven, otherwise the muffins will not rise properly. If the oven temperature is too high, the muffins' tops will be uneven and often cracked. If the oven temperature is too low, then the muffins' tops will not be fully rounded but will have a little dip in the centre. Generally muffins are baked at between 180 °C and 200 °C.

● Grease the tins before adding the batter, or use a paper cup. Fill any unused muffin tins with water while baking.

● Some muffins, particularly those with fruit in them, should be left to stand about three minutes after they have come out of the oven so that they can be turned out of the tin more easily.

● You might need to adjust your flour and liquid proportions — too much liquid and the muffin will be soggy and probably spread all over the muffin tin; too much flour and the muffins will be hard and dry.

● To make sour milk: Combine 1 c milk with 1 T lemon juice or vinegar, stir, and use after about a minute.

● When microwaving bran muffins, mix the oil and bran first, then mix it with the rest of the ingredients to give a moister muffin.

● You may notice that in this book almost all of the recipes call for only baking powder, not both baking powder and soda. This is mostly because of my personal preference — I hate the feeling you get on your teeth if the soda isn't quite all used up in the baking. Both baking powder and soda are there for their leavening qualities. It is said that using soda will give a finer crumb consistency to the muffin. I've never found this to be a problem. If you feel you want to incorporate it in the recipes, then as a general rule use ½ t soda and ½ t powder to every 2 c flour.

Baking muffins is easy, so let's get going!

Muffin recipes A to Z

Almond muffins

The sliced almonds scattered throughout these muffins give them a lovely crunch.

1	egg
1 c	yoghurt
2 t	almond extract
¼ c	margarine
1⅓ c	flour
½ c	sugar
1 T	baking powder
1 c	sliced almonds
12	whole almonds

Lightly oil a muffin tin and preheat the oven to 190 °C. This recipe makes 12 muffins.

Put the first four ingredients into a bowl and mix well, then add the remaining ingredients, except for the whole almonds, and blend until just mixed. Two-thirds fill the muffin tins and place an almond in the centre of each. Bake for 20–25 min.

Almond-centre muffins

These combine a light muffin with a delicious marzipan centre.

150 g	cream cheese
1	egg white
3 T	sugar
2 c	ground almonds
2	eggs
1 c	sour cream
½ c	sugar
1 t	almond extract
1½ c	flour
3 t	baking powder
1 t	cardamom

Lightly oil a muffin tin and preheat the oven to 190 °C. This recipe makes 12 muffins.

Mix the first four ingredients together to make a paste and set aside. Put the next four ingredients in a bowl and mix well, then add the remaining ingredients and blend until just mixed. Two-thirds fill the muffin tins and drop a ball of the almond paste into each. Bake for 15–20 min.

Almond liqueur muffins

Something a little more daring. The amaretto brings out the flavour of the almonds in this recipe. Very nice served with a little extra amaretto drizzled over the top.

⅔ c	sour milk (see page 5)
3 T	melted butter or margarine
1	egg
½ c	amaretto liqueur
1 c	sliced almonds
2 t	baking powder
½ c	sugar
2 c	flour

Lightly oil a muffin tin and preheat the oven to 200 °C. This recipe makes 12 muffins.
Put the first five ingredients into a bowl and mix well, then add the remaining ingredients and blend until just mixed. Two-thirds fill the muffin tins and bake for 15–20 min.

Apple muffins

Slices of apple give this muffin a nice variation of texture. It is particularly successful with Granny Smith apples.

125 g	butter, melted
¼ c	sugar
1	egg
1 c	milk
1 c	apple, peeled, cored and thinly sliced
1 t	cinnamon
2 c	flour
4 t	baking powder

Lightly oil a muffin tin and preheat the oven to 190 °C. This recipe makes 12 muffins.
Put the first four ingredients into a bowl and mix well. Add the apple and stir, then add the remaining ingredients and mix until just blended. Two-thirds fill the muffin tins. Sprinkle a little sugar and cinnamon on top of each muffin and bake for 15–20 min.

Applesauce muffins

An apple a day keeps the doctor away. These muffins are moist and full of spicy apple. I suggest you make up a batch and invite your doctor over for a cup of tea.

1 c	applesauce
½ c	margarine, melted
½ c	brown sugar
1⅓ c	flour
1 t	baking soda
1 t	ground cinnamon
½ t	ground cloves

Lightly oil the muffin tin and preheat the oven to 190 °C. This recipe makes 12 muffins.

Put the first three ingredients into a bowl and mix well. Add the remaining ingredients and blend just until mixed. Two-thirds fill the muffin tins with the batter and bake for 20–25 min.

Cashmere apple muffins

Lois introduced me to this delightfully moist and healthy muffin on a sunny winter's day in Cashmere. I loved the sound of Cashmere and I loved the taste of her muffins, so the logical conclusion was to combine the two.

1	egg
60 g	margarine or butter
1 c	applesauce
¾ c	sugar
1 t	cinnamon
1 t	mixed spice
1½ c	wholemeal flour
1 t	baking powder

Lightly oil the muffin tin and preheat the oven to 190 °C. This recipe makes 15 muffins.

Put the first six ingredients into a bowl and mix well. Add the remaining ingredients and blend until just mixed. Two-thirds fill the muffin tins with the batter and bake for 15 min.

Eve's apple muffins

Eve has always been full of surprises and her muffins are no exception.

The naughty bits on top
100 g	butter
¼ c	sugar
1 c	flour
1 t	baking powder
1 t	ground cinnamon

Mix these all together, form into a ball and refrigerate until required.

The yummy bits in the middle
1	egg
¼ c	sour milk (see page 5)
¼ c	oil
1 c	apple, cored and chopped but not peeled
1½ c	flour
½ c	sugar
3 t	baking powder

Lightly oil a muffin tin and preheat the oven to 200 °C. This recipe makes 12 muffins.

Put the first four ingredients into a bowl, mix well, then add the remaining three ingredients and blend until just mixed. Two-thirds fill the muffin tins and grate a little of the topping over each muffin. Bake for 15–20 min.

Fudgy apple muffins

These are delicious! I love chocolate and I love apples — what could be better?

60 g	cooking chocolate
125 g	butter, melted
1 c	applesauce
2	eggs
¾ c	brown sugar
1 t	vanilla
1 c	flour
1½ t	baking powder
½ c	chopped walnuts (optional)

Lightly oil a muffin tin and preheat the oven to 190 °C. This recipe makes 14 muffins.

Melt the chocolate and butter, then allow to cool. Add the next four ingredients and mix well. Add the remaining ingredients and mix until just blended. Two-thirds fill the muffin tins and bake for 15–20 min.

Oat-bran apple muffins

Great for the cholesterol-conscious. The soluble fibre from the rolled oats and the oat bran is said to be helpful in keeping down cholesterol. If you are being cholesterol-conscious be sure to use margarine instead of butter and use only the egg white, not the yolk.

1 c	applesauce
50 g	margarine, melted
1	egg
½ c	sugar
½ t	five-spice powder
1 t	baking powder
1 c	flour
1 c	oat bran
¾ c	rolled oats

Lightly oil a muffin tin and preheat the oven to 200 °C. This recipe makes 12 muffins.
Put the first five ingredients into a bowl and mix well. Add the remaining ingredients and blend until just mixed. Two-thirds fill the muffin tins and bake for 10–15 min.

Apple raisin muffins

Crisp, sweet apples and plump, juicy raisins — what a combo!

1½ c	apples, peeled, cored and chopped
1 c	raisins
2 T	sherry
½ c	sugar
2	eggs
¾ c	cream
½ c	margarine, softened
2 t	mixed spice
2 c	flour
3 t	baking powder

Lightly oil the muffin tin and preheat the oven to 200 °C. This recipe makes 15 muffins.
Put the first three ingredients into a bowl and set aside.
Put the next three ingredients into another bowl and mix well. Add the remaining ingredients plus the apple mixture and blend just until it is mixed. Two-thirds fill the muffin tins with the batter and bake for 15–20 min.

Surprise applesauce muffins

These must be allowed to stand for a few minutes after baking so that the 'surprise' doesn't fall out as you lift the muffin from the tin.

½ c	applesauce
½ t	cinnamon
2	eggs
2 T	margarine, softened
1 c	sour milk (see page 5) or yoghurt
1½ c	flour
½ c	sugar
2 t	baking powder
½ t	freshly grated root ginger
½ t	ground cinnamon
¾ t	allspice
	grated rind of 1 lemon

Lightly oil a muffin tin and preheat the oven to 200 °C. This recipe makes 12 muffins.

Mix the applesauce and cinnamon together and set aside. Put the eggs, margarine and milk into a bowl and mix well. Add the remaining ingredients (but not the applesauce mixture) and blend until just mixed. Fill the muffin tins a third full of batter, then spoon a teaspoon of the applesauce mixture into the middle of each. Cover with the remaining batter and bake for 15–20 min.

Be sure to let these cool slightly before you remove them from the tin.

Wholemeal apple muffins

This recipe gives you what's good for you — fruit and bran baked in a tasty muffin.

2	eggs
1 c	applesauce
¼ c	margarine
1½ c	wholemeal flour
½ c	brown sugar
½ c	oat bran
½ c	rolled oats
1 t	ground cinnamon
½ t	ground nutmeg
2 t	baking powder
1 c	chopped walnuts

Lightly oil a muffin tin and preheat the oven to 190 °C. This recipe makes 12 muffins.

Put the first three ingredients into a bowl and mix well. Add the remaining ingredients and blend until just mixed. Two-thirds fill the muffin tins, sprinkle tops with a little brown sugar and bake for 15–20 min.

Apricot muffins

The zing of apricots comes out well in these muffins.

1 c	apricot puree
1 c	dried apricots, chopped
½ c	milk
½ c	yoghurt
¼ c	oil
½ c	sugar
2	eggs
1 t	vanilla
1¾ c	flour
1¼ T	baking powder

Lightly oil a muffin tin and preheat the oven to 200 °C. This recipe makes 15 muffins.

Put the first eight ingredients into a bowl and mix well. Add the remaining ingredients and mix until just blended. Two-thirds fill the muffin tins and bake for 15–20 min.

Plain apricot muffins

This gives a lighter apricot flavour than the previous recipe. The bits of dried apricot tingle the taste buds.

1 c	chopped dried apricots
4 T	butter, melted
¾ c	milk
2	eggs
1¾ c	flour
¼ c	sugar
3 t	baking powder

Lightly oil a muffin tin and preheat the oven to 200 °C. This recipe makes 15 muffins.

Put the first four ingredients into a bowl and mix well, then add the remaining ingredients and mix until just blended. Two-thirds fill the muffin tins and bake for 15–20 min.

Bacon muffins

Great for breakfast, lunch or dinner!

2 T	bacon fat
1 c	milk
1	egg
2 T	sugar
3 t	baking powder
2 c	flour
3	rashers bacon, chopped and fried

Lightly oil a muffin tin and preheat the oven to 200 °C. This recipe makes 12 muffins.

Put the first three ingredients into a bowl and mix well. Add all remaining ingredients except the bacon, blend until just mixed, then fold in the bacon. Two-thirds fill the muffin tins and bake for 15–20 min.

Banana almond muffins

Almond and banana complement each other well here.

¼ c	sour milk (see page 5)
⅓ c	margarine, softened
2	eggs
2	bananas, mashed
½ t	almond extract
1 c	flour
¾ c	sugar
1½ t	baking powder
1 c	almonds, sliced and toasted

Lightly oil a muffin tin and preheat the oven to 190 °C. This recipe makes 12 muffins.

Put the first five ingredients into a bowl and mix well, then add the remaining ingredients and mix until just blended. Two-thirds fill the muffin tins, place a slice or two of almond on top and bake for 15–20 min.

Banana bran muffins

You don't really need any excuses to make this very nice bran muffin recipe.

3 T	oil
3 T	golden syrup
1 c	milk or yoghurt
1	large banana, mashed
1 c	bran
1 c	flour
1½ t	baking powder

Lightly oil a muffin tin and preheat the oven to 200 °C. This recipe makes 12 muffins.

Heat together the oil and golden syrup, remove it from the heat and add the yoghurt. Put the banana into a bowl and mash well. Add the oil mixture and mix well, then add the remaining ingredients and mix until just blended. Two-thirds fill the muffin tins and bake for 12–15 min.

Lemon and banana muffins

2	eggs
2	bananas, mashed
¼ t	lemon rind, grated
1 t	lemon juice
3 T	yoghurt
3 T	margarine, softened
3 T	sugar
1¾ t	baking powder
1½ c	flour

Lightly oil a muffin tin and preheat the oven to 200 °C. This recipe makes 12 muffins.

Put the first seven ingredients into a bowl and mix well, then add the remaining ingredients and blend until just mixed. Two-thirds fill the muffin tins and bake for 10–15 min.

Banana and oat-bran muffins

There are lots of versions of this popular muffin but I think this is the best of them.

1	egg
5 T	melted butter or margarine
¾ c	yoghurt
2	bananas, mashed
1 t	vanilla essence
¾ c	brown sugar
1 c	flour
1 c	oat bran
1¼ t	baking powder

Lightly oil a muffin tin and preheat the oven to 200 °C. This recipe makes 12 muffins.

Put the first six ingredients into a bowl and mix well, then add the remaining ingredients and blend until just mixed. Two-thirds fill the muffin tins and bake for 15–20 min.

Banana pecan muffins

Moist and tasty because of the banana, and crunchy because of the pecan, these muffins are delicious any time of the day.

2	bananas, mashed
1	egg
¼ c	yoghurt
½ c	sugar
1½ c	flour
2½ t	baking powder
¼ t	ground cardamom
1 c	pecans, chopped

Lightly oil a muffin tin and preheat the oven to 190 °C. This recipe makes 15 muffins.

Put the first four ingredients into a bowl and mix well. Add the remaining ingredients and blend until just mixed. Two-thirds fill the muffin tins and bake for 20–25 min.

Rolled oats and banana muffins

I love the texture that the rolled oats give to this banana muffin.

3 T	margarine, softened
2	large bananas, mashed
1	egg
½ c	sugar
1 t	baking powder
1 c	flour
1 c	oat bran
¾ c	rolled oats
1 t	cinnamon

Lightly oil the muffin tin and preheat the oven to 200 °C. This recipe makes 12 muffins.
Put the first four ingredients into a bowl and mix well. Add the remaining ingredients and blend until just mixed. Two-thirds fill the muffin tins and bake for 10–15 min.

Tropical banana muffins

You like banana? You like pineapple? Then you will probably like this muffin too!

2	bananas, mashed
⅔ c	yoghurt
⅔ c	margarine, softened
3	eggs
¾ c	pineapple pieces, well drained and roughly chopped
2½ c	flour
¾ c	sugar
2½ t	baking powder

Lightly oil a muffin tin and preheat the oven to 190 °C. This recipe makes 24 muffins.
Put the bananas into a bowl and mash well. Add the next four ingredients and mix well, then add the remaining ingredients and mix until just blended. Two-thirds fill the muffin tins and bake for 20–25 min.

Banana yoghurt muffins

This makes a richer banana muffin than the preceding recipe because of the brown sugar and yoghurt.

¼ c	yoghurt
½ c	margarine, softened
2	eggs
1¼ c	brown sugar
2 or 3	bananas, mashed
1¾ c	flour
1 t	baking powder

Lightly oil a muffin tin and preheat the oven to 200 °C. This recipe makes 15 muffins.

Put the first five ingredients into a bowl and mix well. Add the remaining ingredients and mix until just blended. Two-thirds fill the muffin tins and bake for 20–25 min.

Basic muffin

This is a good all-round muffin that is nice just as it is, or you can experiment with the recipe by adding anything you like.

1	egg
1 c	milk
2 T	oil
¼ c	sugar
4 t	baking powder
2 c	flour

Lightly oil a muffin tin and preheat the oven to 190 °C. This recipe makes 12 muffins.

Put the first four ingredients into a bowl and mix well, then add the remaining ingredients and blend until just mixed. Two-thirds fill the muffin tins and bake for 15–20 min.

Blueberry muffins

This is a genuine American recipe from my friend Janice in Idaho. It is a good, tasty blueberry muffin recipe worth trying.

1	egg
½ c	milk
½ c	yoghurt
4 T	melted butter
⅓ c	sugar
2½ t	baking powder
2½ c	flour
1 c	blueberries

Lightly oil a muffin tin and preheat the oven to 190 °C. This recipe makes 12 muffins.

Put the first four ingredients into a bowl and mix well. Add the remaining ingredients except the berries and blend until just mixed, then fold in the blueberries. Two-thirds fill the muffin tins and bake for 15–20 min.

The classic blueberry muffin

Remember that you might need to let these stand in their tins a few minutes after cooking so the fruit stays in the muffins when you turn them out.

1	egg
¾ c	milk
⅓ c	oil
1¾ c	flour
¾ t	salt
¼ c	sugar
2½ t	baking powder
2 T	lemon rind
¾ c	blueberries

Lightly oil a muffin tin and preheat the oven to 200 °C. This recipe makes 12 muffins.

Put the first three ingredients into a bowl and mix well. Add the remaining ingredients except the blueberries and blend until just mixed, then fold in the blueberries. Two-thirds fill the muffin tins and bake for 15–20 min.

Blueberry cornmeal muffins

Since these muffins have whole fruit in them, let them stand in their tins for a few minutes after cooking.

1	egg
½ c	sour milk (see page 5) or yoghurt
½ c	butter or margarine
1 c	flour
1 c	finely ground cornmeal
¼ c	sugar
2 t	baking powder
1 c	blueberries

Lightly oil a muffin tin and preheat the oven to 210 °C. This recipe makes 12 muffins.

Put the first three ingredients into a bowl and mix well. Add all remaining ingredients except the blueberries and blend until just mixed, then fold in the blueberries. Two-thirds fill the muffin tins and bake for 15–20 min.

The basic bran muffin

This is a 'go anywhere, do anything' muffin.

3 T	oil
3 T	golden syrup
1 c	milk
1 c	flour
1 c	bran
1 t	baking powder

Lightly oil a muffin tin and preheat the oven to 200 °C. This recipe makes 12 muffins.

Heat together the golden syrup and the oil until they just come to a boil, remove from the heat and add the milk. In another bowl put the remaining ingredients, add the liquid and mix until just blended. Two-thirds fill the muffin tins and bake for 10–15 min.

Date bran muffins

Raisins or dried apricots can be substituted for the dates in this recipe.

1	egg
1½ c	yoghurt
¼ c	margarine
1½ c	bran
2 c	chopped dates
1¾ c	flour
1 T	baking powder
⅓ c	sugar

Lightly oil a muffin tin and preheat the oven to 190 °C. This recipe makes 12 muffins.

Put the first five ingredients into a bowl and mix well, then add the remaining ingredients and blend until just mixed. Two-thirds fill the muffin tins and bake for 15–20 min.

Molasses bran muffins

Blackstrap molasses gives these muffins a good strong flavour and colour.

2 c	bran
½ c	oil
½ c	molasses
2	eggs
2 ½ c	yoghurt
1 c	raisins
2½ c	flour
3 t	baking powder

Lightly oil a muffin tin and preheat the oven to 200 °C. This recipe makes 18 muffins.

Mix the bran and the oil together. Add the molasses, eggs and yoghurt and mix well. Add the raisins, flour and baking powder and blend until just mixed. Two-thirds fill the muffin tins and bake for 15–20 min.

The basic oat-bran muffin

This muffin has a little more class — it's probably the oats.

3 T	margarine, softened
1	egg
½ c	sugar
½ c	yoghurt
1 t	baking powder
1 c	flour
1 c	oat bran
¾ c	rolled oats
2 t	mixed spice

Lightly oil a muffin tin and preheat the oven to 200 °C. This recipe makes 12 muffins.

Put the first four ingredients into a bowl and mix well. Add the remaining ingredients and blend until just mixed. Two-thirds fill the muffin tins and bake for 10–15 min.

Mrs Pudwaka's bran muffins

These have been known to be consumed in great quantities by groups of hungry, hard-working types.

3 c	bran
1 c	boiling water
½ c	margarine, melted
1½ c	sugar
2	eggs
2 c	buttermilk or yoghurt
2½ c	flour
2½ t	soda
1 t	salt

Lightly oil the muffin tin and preheat the oven to 190 °C. This recipe makes 20 muffins.
Put the bran into a bowl, cover with the water and let it stand for about 10 min.
Put the next four ingredients into a bowl, mix well, add the bran and mix again.
Add the remaining ingredients and blend until just mixed. Two-thirds fill the muffin tins and bake for 15–20 min.

Low-cholesterol oat-bran muffins

Watching your cholesterol isn't at all difficult when you can make muffins like this to have with a cup of tea.

2 c	low-fat yoghurt
3 T	oil
3	egg whites
½ c	sugar
2 c	rolled oats
1 c	oat bran
1½ c	flour
2½ T	baking powder
2 t	cinnamon

Lightly oil a muffin tin and preheat the oven to 190 °C. This recipe makes 20 muffins.
Put the first four ingredients into a bowl and mix well. Add the remaining ingredients and blend until just mixed. Two-thirds fill the muffin tins and bake for 20–25 min.

Even lower cholesterol oat-bran muffins

Just when you thought life couldn't get any better, along comes this muffin to tantalise your taste buds.

1½ c	low-fat milk
2 T	oil
2	egg whites
2	bananas, mashed
2½ c	oat bran
1 T	baking powder
½ c	chopped walnuts
½ c	brown sugar

Lightly oil a muffin tin and preheat the oven to 180 °C. This recipe makes 12 muffins.
Put the first four ingredients in a bowl and mix well. Add the remaining ingredients and blend until just mixed. Two-thirds fill the muffin tins and bake for 15–20 min.

Maple syrup oat-bran muffins

If you can get hold of real maple syrup for this muffin, it is worth it.

2⅓ c	sour milk (see page 5) or yoghurt
2	eggs
3 T	oil
⅔ c	maple syrup
½ c	oat bran
2 c	flour
2½ T	baking powder
1 c	chopped pecans
3 c	rolled oats

Lightly oil a muffin tin and preheat the oven to 190 °C. This recipe makes 20 muffins.

Put the first four ingredients into a bowl and mix well. Add the remaining ingredients and blend until just mixed. Two-thirds fill the muffin tins and bake for 15–20 min.

Spicy oat-bran muffins

Apples, spice and bran, what a great combination — healthy and filling.

1 c	applesauce
½ c	brown sugar
1½ c	yoghurt
2	eggs
3 T	oil
1 c	oat bran
½ c	rolled oats
½ c	wholemeal flour
1 c	white flour
½ t	five-spice powder
1 c	chopped nuts (optional)

Lightly oil a muffin tin and preheat the oven to 200 °C. This recipe makes 20 muffins.

Put the first five ingredients into a bowl and mix well, then add the remaining ingredients and blend until just mixed. Two-thirds fill the muffin tins and bake for 15–20 min.

Cabbage muffins

This is a very nice savoury muffin to have with soup or as an accompaniment to roast pork.

3 T	melted margarine
2	eggs
1 c	milk
2 T	grated onion
2 c	grated cabbage
2 t	celery seed
1 T	sugar
1 t	salt
1 T	baking powder
1¾ c	flour

Lightly oil a muffin tin and preheat the oven to 200 °C. This recipe makes 12 muffins.
Put the first eight ingredients into a bowl and mix well. Add the remaining ingredients and blend until just mixed. Two-thirds fill the muffin tins and bake for 15–20 min.

Carrot muffins

Don't be put off by the vegetable content — think of that delicious carrot cake you had last week!

1 c	milk
1	egg
3 T	margarine
1 c	grated carrots
½ c	raisins
1 t	cinnamon
1 t	nutmeg
2½ t	baking powder
¼ c	brown sugar
1¾ c	flour

Lightly oil a muffin tin and preheat the oven to 190 °C. This recipe makes 12 muffins.
Put the first seven ingredients into a bowl and mix well. Then add the remaining ingredients and blend until just mixed. Two-thirds fill the muffin tins and bake for 15 min.

Carrot and apple muffins

Colours and flavours combine well in this muffin.

1 c	grated and peeled apple
1½ c	grated carrot
1½ c	sour cream
1 c	brown sugar
2	eggs
2 t	vanilla
2½ c	flour
1 T	baking powder

Lightly oil a muffin tin and preheat the oven to 190 °C. This recipe makes 20 muffins.

Put the first six ingredients into a bowl and mix well. Add the remaining ingredients and blend until just mixed. Two-thirds fill the muffin tins and bake for 20–25 min.

Curry carrot muffins

These are tending toward the savoury sort of muffin but are not altogether removed from the sweet type.

1½ c	sugar
1 c	oil
3	eggs
2 c	grated carrot
3 c	flour
3 t	baking powder
½ t	turmeric
½ t	curry powder
1 c	pistachio nuts

Lightly oil a muffin tin and preheat the oven to 200 °C. This recipe makes 24 muffins.

Put the first four ingredients into a bowl and mix well. Add the remaining ingredients and blend until just mixed. Two-thirds fill the muffin tins and bake for 15–20 min.

Carrot rice muffins

This may sound like a savoury muffin but it isn't really. The rice and sesame seeds give it an interesting texture.

2	eggs
1 c	milk
1 T	melted butter
½ c	sesame seeds
½ c	cooked rice
1 c	grated carrot
1½ c	flour
1 T	brown sugar
2 t	baking powder

Lightly oil a muffin tin and preheat the oven to 200 °C. This recipe makes 12 muffins.
Put the first six ingredients into a bowl and mix well. Add the remaining ingredients and blend until they are just mixed. Two-thirds fill the muffin tins and bake for 20–25 min.

Cheese muffins

This is a delicious savoury muffin to serve any time.

1 c	milk
3 T	melted butter
1	egg
1 c	grated cheese
½ t	salt
1 T	baking powder
2 c	flour

Lightly oil a muffin tin and preheat the oven to 200 °C. This recipe makes 12 muffins.
Put the first three ingredients into a bowl and mix well. Add the remaining ingredients and blend until just mixed. Two-thirds fill the muffin tins and sprinkle a little extra grated cheese over the top of each muffin. Bake for 15–20 min.

Fondue cheese muffins

A bit more than just a cheese muffin!

1	egg
1 c	milk
3 T	melted margarine
3 T	kirsch
1 c	grated gruyere cheese
1	clove garlic, crushed
½ t	nutmeg
3 t	baking powder
2 c	flour

Lightly oil a muffin tin and preheat the oven to 190 °C. This recipe makes 12 muffins.
Put the first four ingredients into a bowl and mix well. Add the remaining ingredients and blend until just mixed. Two-thirds fill the muffin tins and bake for 15–20 min.

Rye-flour cheese muffins

The rye flour makes this a heavier muffin, but the flavours are great.

1	egg
½ c	oil
1½ c	yoghurt
2 t	worcestershire sauce
1½ c	grated tasty cheese
2 t	baking powder
3 T	sugar
½ c	rye flour
1½ c	flour

Lightly oil a muffin tin and preheat the oven to 200 °C. This recipe makes 12 muffins.
Put the first four ingredients into a bowl and mix well. Add the remaining ingredients and blend until just mixed. Two-thirds fill the muffin tins and bake for 15–20 min.

Cherry muffins

These are nice with fresh cherries, too; but you'll have to stone them first or face the possibility of big dental bills...

1⅓ c	yoghurt
2 T	melted margarine or butter
1	egg
½ t	cinnamon
2 t	baking powder
⅓ c	sugar
1½ c	flour
1½ c	Bing cherries, tinned

Lightly oil a muffin tin and preheat the oven to 200 °C. This recipe makes 12 muffins.
Put the first four ingredients into a bowl and mix well. Add the remaining ingredients except the cherries and blend until just mixed, then fold in the cherries, but do not overmix. Two-thirds fill the muffin tins and bake for 15–20 min.

Cherry almond muffins

Try these with other sorts of nut too like pecans or walnuts. The flavours all combine well.

2	eggs
2 T	sugar
1 t	almond essence
¼ c	oil
1½ c	cherry jam
1 c	slivered almonds
4 t	baking powder
2 c	flour

Lightly oil a muffin tin and preheat the oven to 190 °C. This recipe makes 14 muffins.
Put the first five ingredients into a bowl and mix well. Add the remaining ingredients and blend until just mixed. Two-thirds fill the muffin tins and bake for 15–20 min.

Chocolate cherry muffins

1	egg
1 t	vanilla
⅓ c	white sugar
⅔ c	brown sugar
1 c	sour cream or yoghurt
½ c	melted margarine or butter
60 g	cooking chocolate, melted
1½ c	flour
1¼ t	baking powder
1 c	drained Bing cherries, tinned

Lightly oil a muffin tin and preheat the oven to 190 °C. This recipe makes 15 muffins.

Put the first seven ingredients into a bowl and mix well, then add the remaining ingredients except the cherries and blend until just mixed. Fold in the cherries, but do not overmix. Two-thirds fill the muffin tins and bake for 15–20 min.

Chocolate-chip muffins

If you like chocolate-chip cookies then you'll like these muffins, and so will the kids.

1	egg
½ c	milk
1 c	yoghurt
½ c	melted butter
1 t	vanilla
1 c	chopped walnuts
1 c	chocolate chips
3 t	baking powder
⅓ c	white sugar
⅔ c	brown sugar
2 c	flour

Lightly oil a muffin tin and preheat the oven to 190 °C. This recipe makes 16 muffins.

Put the first five ingredients into a bowl and mix well, then add the remaining ingredients and blend until just mixed. Two-thirds fill the muffin tins and bake for 15–20 min.

Chocolate cream muffins

Maybe this is what you've been looking for?

130 g	cream cheese
1 T	cocoa
2	eggs
1 c	yoghurt
½ c	sugar
1 t	vanilla
3 t	baking powder
1¾ c	flour

Lightly oil a muffin tin and preheat the oven to 190 °C. This recipe makes 12 muffins.
Put the first six ingredients into a bowl and cream together. Add the remaining ingredients and blend until just mixed. Two-thirds fill the muffin tins and bake for 15–20 min.

Nutty chocolate and marshmallow muffins

These are for all those chocolate freaks out there!

60 g	cooking chocolate, melted
½ c	melted butter or margarine
1 c	sour cream or yoghurt
½ c	brown sugar
1	egg
1 t	vanilla
1½ c	flour
1 t	baking powder
½ c	chopped walnuts
¾ c	chopped marshmallows

Lightly oil a muffin tin and preheat the oven to 200 °C. This recipe makes 15 muffins.
Put the first six ingredients into a bowl and mix well. Add the remaining ingredients except the marshmallows, blend until just mixed, then fold in the marshmallows. Two-thirds fill the muffin tins and bake for 15–20 min.

Cinnamon muffins

Really yummy, probably my favourite muffin!

½ c	milk
½ c	yoghurt
4 T	melted margarine
1	egg
½ c	sugar
2 t	cinnamon
2 t	baking powder
1½ c	flour

Lightly oil a muffin tin and preheat the oven to 200 °C. This recipe makes 12 muffins.

Put the first six ingredients into a bowl and mix well. Add the remaining ingredients and blend until just mixed. Two-thirds fill the muffin tins and bake for 15–20 min.

Cocoa muffins

Three cheers for the inventor of cocoa! It makes these quick and easy muffins so moist and chocolatey, too!

1¼ c	yoghurt
½ c	margarine, melted
2	eggs
½ c	cocoa
⅔ c	sugar
1 c	raisins
1 T	baking powder
2¼ c	flour

Lightly oil the muffin tin and preheat the oven to 200 °C. This recipe makes 24 muffins.

Put the first five ingredients into a bowl and mix well, then add the remaining ingredients and blend until just mixed. Two-thirds fill the muffin tins and bake for 15–20 min.

Cocoa almond muffins

Almonds give the texture a lift in this muffin.

1	egg
2 T	melted margarine
1¼ c	sour cream or yoghurt
1 t	vanilla
½ c	sugar
¼ c	cocoa
½ c	slivered almonds
2 t	baking powder
1½ c	flour

Lightly oil a muffin tin and preheat the oven to 200 °C. This recipe makes 12 muffins.
Put the first six ingredients into a bowl and mix well, then add the remaining ingredients and blend until just mixed. Two-thirds fill the muffin tins and bake for 15–20 min.

Cocoa apple muffins

Great with mugs of cocoa for the kids after school.

¼ c	margarine, melted
4 t	cocoa
¾ c	applesauce
1 c	sugar
1	egg
1 t	five-spice powder
1¼ c	flour
1 t	baking powder

Lightly oil a muffin tin and preheat the oven to 190 °C. This recipe makes 12 muffins.
Put the first six ingredients into a bowl and mix well, then add the remaining ingredients and blend until just mixed. Two-thirds fill the muffin tins and bake for 15–20 min.

Coconut muffins

These non-aggressive muffins are light and moist. If you can get hold of a fresh coconut and shred your own, they are even better.

2	eggs
4 T	melted margarine
¼ c	white wine
⅔ c	yoghurt
1 t	grated orange rind
1½ c	coarsely shredded coconut
½ c	sugar
2 t	baking powder
1½ c	flour

Lightly oil a muffin tin and preheat the oven to 200 °C. This recipe makes 12 muffins.

Put the first seven ingredients into a bowl and mix well. Add the remaining ingredients and blend until just mixed. Two-thirds fill the muffin tins and bake for 15–20 min.

Coconut-cream muffins

You really get the flavour of the coconut with these muffins.

2	eggs
1 T	rum
3 T	melted margarine
1 c	coconut cream
1 c	coarsely shredded coconut
¾ c	chopped pineapple
2 t	baking powder
½ c	sugar
1¾ c	flour

Lightly oil a muffin tin and preheat the oven to 200 °C. This recipe makes 12 muffins.

Put the first six ingredients into a bowl and mix well. Add the remaining ingredients and blend until just mixed. Two-thirds fill the muffin tins, sprinkle a little coconut on top of each muffin and bake for 15–20 min.

Coconut and rolled-oat muffins

Great served with piping hot coffee or tea with a squeeze of lemon.

2	eggs
1½ c	yoghurt
½ c	oil
1 c	mashed banana
½ c	brown sugar
2½ t	baking powder
1½ c	flour
2 c	rolled oats
1¼ c	coconut

Lightly oil a muffin tin and preheat the oven to 190 °C. This recipe makes 18 muffins.

Put the first five ingredients into a bowl and mix well. Add the remaining ingredients and blend until just mixed. Two-thirds fill the muffin tins and bake for 20–25 min.

Corn muffins

Serve these with soup on a winter's day for an easy and tasty lunch.

1	egg
2 T	melted margarine or butter
1¼ c	sour milk (see page 5)
2 T	sugar
1 c	whole corn, drained
2 t	baking powder
1½ c	flour

Lightly oil a muffin tin and preheat the oven to 200 °C. This recipe makes 12 muffins.

Put the first five ingredients into a bowl and mix well. Add the remaining ingredients and blend until mixed. Two-thirds fill the muffin tin and bake for 15–20 min.

Cornbread muffins

I got this recipe from a Southern Belle who always serves them with fried chicken.

⅓ c	margarine, melted
¼ c	sugar
1¼ c	milk
1	egg
1 c	flour
½ c	fine cornmeal
½ c	coarse cornmeal
4 t	baking powder

Lightly oil a muffin tin and preheat the oven to 200 °C. This recipe makes 12 muffins.

Put the first four ingredients into a bowl and mix well. Add the remaining ingredients and blend until just mixed. Two-thirds fill the muffin tins and bake for 20–25 min.

Cornmeal, bacon and onion muffins

A more substantial muffin of the savoury persuasion.

3	rashers bacon, chopped
1 c	chopped onion
1 T	oil
2	eggs
1 T	honey
1 c	yoghurt
1 c	milk
3 T	tomato sauce
1½ t	baking powder
½ c	flour
1 c	fine cornmeal
1 c	coarse cornmeal

Lightly oil a muffin tin and preheat the oven to 190 °C. This recipe makes 12 muffins.

Fry the bacon and onion together until the onion is transparent and the bacon is just beginning to crisp. Put the oil, eggs, honey, yoghurt, milk and tomato sauce into a bowl and mix well. Add the bacon and onion mixture and mix, then add the remaining ingredients and blend until just mixed. Two-thirds fill the muffin tins and bake for 15–20 min.

Cornmeal and cheese muffins

Hearty texture and yummy flavour make these muffins special.

1 c	milk
1 c	yoghurt
1 T	oil
1 T	honey
2	eggs
1 c	coarse cornmeal
1 c	fine cornmeal
½ c	flour
1½ t	baking powder
1 c	grated tasty cheese

Lightly oil a muffin tin and preheat the oven to 190 °C. This recipe makes 12 muffins.

Put the first five ingredients into a bowl and mix well. Add the remaining ingredients and blend until just mixed. Two-thirds fill the muffin tins and bake for 20–25 min.

Cornmeal and chilli muffins

You can usually get these chillies in cans or jars from a delicatessen.

2 c	yoghurt
1 T	honey
1 T	oil
2	eggs
60 g	jalapeno chillies, tinned
2 t	baking powder
½ c	flour
1 c	fine cornmeal
1 c	coarse cornmeal

Lightly oil a muffin tin and preheat the oven to 190 °C. This recipe makes 15 muffins.

Put the first four ingredients into a bowl and mix well. Add the remaining ingredients and blend until just mixed. Two-thirds fill the muffin tins and bake for 15–20 min.

Whole-kernel corn and cornmeal muffins

Real 'down-country' muffins.

½ c	melted margarine or butter
1¼ c	yoghurt
2	eggs
½ c	chopped green and red capsicum
1 c	drained whole-kernel corn
½ c	sugar
4 t	baking powder
1 c	flour
1 c	fine cornmeal

Lightly oil a muffin tin and preheat the oven to 200 °C. This recipe makes 18 muffins.

Put the first six ingredients into a bowl and mix well. Add the remaining ingredients and blend until just mixed. Two-thirds fill the muffin tins and bake for 20–25 min.

Cornmeal ham muffins

A very nice savoury muffin.

¼ c	milk
¼ c	oil
1 c	yoghurt
2	eggs
1 c	chopped, cooked ham
2½ t	baking powder
3 t	dry mustard
½ c	coarse cornmeal
1 c	flour

Lightly oil a muffin tin and preheat the oven to 190 °C. This recipe makes 12 muffins.

Put the first five ingredients into a bowl and mix well. Add the remaining ingredients and blend until just mixed. Two-thirds fill the muffin tins and bake for 15–20 min.

Toad-in-the-hole cornmeal muffins

These are great for picnics and school lunches.

1¼ c	milk
1	egg
⅓ c	margarine, melted
1 T	sugar
4 t	baking powder
1 c	flour
1 c	fine cornmeal
15	cocktail sausages (cheerios)

Lightly oil a muffin tin and preheat the oven to 200 °C. This recipe makes 15 muffins.

Put the first four ingredients into a bowl and mix well. Add the remaining ingredients except the sausages and blend until just mixed. Two-thirds fill the muffin tins and pop a sausage into the middle of each muffin. The mixture should be firm enough to hold up the sausages. Bake for 15-20 min.

Cornmeal and wholemeal muffins

This recipe makes a hearty, healthy muffin.

2	eggs
2 c	yoghurt
1 T	honey
1 T	oil
1 t	baking powder
½ c	wholemeal flour
1 c	fine cornmeal
1 c	coarse cornmeal

Lightly oil a muffin tin and preheat the oven to 190 °C. This recipe makes 12 muffins.

Put the first four ingredients into a bowl and mix well. Add the remaining ingredients and blend until just mixed. Two-thirds fill the muffin tins and bake for 15-20 min.

Coffee muffins

Served with jam and freshly brewed coffee, these are delicious.

1 c	very strong black coffee, cold
1 c	sugar
2	eggs
1 c	yoghurt
2½ c	flour
2 t	baking powder

Lightly oil a muffin tin and preheat the oven to 200 °C. This recipe makes 15 muffins.

Put the first four ingredients into a bowl and mix well. Add the remaining ingredients and blend until just mixed. Two-thirds fill the muffin tins and bake for 15–20 min.

Courgette muffins

Make these with either green or yellow courgettes or a combination of both, for different visual effects.

1 c	oil
2 c	grated courgettes
1 t	vanilla
¼ c	sherry
4	eggs
1 c	sugar
1 t	cinnamon
2 t	baking powder
3 c	flour

Lightly oil a muffin tin and preheat the oven to 200 °C. This recipe makes 24 muffins.

Put the first seven ingredients into a bowl and mix well. Add the remaining ingredients and blend until just mixed. Two-thirds fill the muffin tins and bake for 15–20 min.

Golden courgette muffins

Colourful and tasty, these muffins will be sure to win applause.

2	eggs
⅔ c	grated carrots
⅔ c	raisins
⅔ c	grated yellow courgette
½ t	vanilla
½ c	melted margarine or butter
¼ t	allspice
½ t	baking powder
1 t	ground coriander
1½ c	flour

Lightly oil a muffin tin and preheat the oven to 190 °C. This recipe makes 12 muffins.

Put the first seven ingredients into a bowl and mix well. Add the remaining ingredients and blend until just mixed. Two-thirds fill the muffin tins and bake for 20–25 min.

Cranberry muffins

Fresh cranberries are often hard to obtain, but if you can get them, this is a nice recipe. Otherwise use tinned cranberries or cranberry jelly, available in grocery stores.

2	eggs
¾ c	yoghurt
4 T	margarine
1 c	chopped cranberries or tinned cranberry jelly
1 t	grated orange rind
⅓ c	sugar
1¾ c	flour
2 t	baking powder

Lightly oil a muffin tin and preheat the oven to 200 °C. This recipe makes 15 muffins.
Put the first six ingredients into a bowl and mix well. Add the remaining ingredients and blend until just mixed. Two-thirds fill the muffin tins and bake for 15–20 min.

Curacao muffins

A lovely strong orange flavour is brought out by the curacao. Definitely one to try.

½ c	melted margarine
¾ c	sugar
¼ c	apple juice
½ c	curacao liqueur
2	eggs
½ c	lemon cheese
2 t	baking powder
1¾ c	flour

Lightly oil a muffin tin and preheat the oven to 190 °C. This recipe makes 20 muffins.
Put the first six ingredients into a bowl and mix well. Add the remaining ingredients and blend until just mixed. Two-thirds fill the muffin tins and bake for 15–20 min.

Currant muffins

Try making these with fresh currants, too, for a taste and texture difference.

1 c	yoghurt
2 T	melted margarine or butter
1	egg
⅓ c	brown sugar
½ t	cinnamon
½ c	raisins
1 c	currants
3 t	baking powder
⅔ c	wholemeal flour
1 c	white flour

Lightly oil a muffin tin and preheat the oven to 200 °C. This recipe makes 12 muffins.
Put the first seven ingredients into a bowl and mix well. Add the remaining ingredients and blend until just mixed. Two-thirds fill the muffin tins and bake for 15–20 min.

Curry muffins

Served with your favourite curry dish, these go down a treat.

3 T	melted margarine or butter
1	egg
1¼ c	yoghurt
⅔ c	shredded coconut
⅔ c	peeled, cored and chopped apples
⅓ c	raisins
¾ t	curry powder
2 t	baking powder
½ c	sugar
1½ c	flour

Lightly oil a muffin tin and preheat the oven to 200 °C. This recipe makes 14 muffins.
Put the first seven ingredients into a bowl and mix well. Add the remaining ingredients and blend until just mixed. Two-thirds fill the muffin tins and bake for 15–20 min.

Date muffins

Fresh dates are great in this recipe, but not all of us are able to obtain them. If using dried dates you might like to soak them first for a while in warm apple juice or sherry.

1 c	milk
1	egg
⅔ c	sugar
1 t	vanilla
½ c	melted butter or margarine
1 c	chopped dates
½ c	chopped walnuts
2¼ c	flour
3 t	baking powder

Lightly oil a muffin tin and preheat the oven to 190 °C. This recipe makes 14 muffins.

Put the first seven ingredients into a bowl and mix well. Add the remaining ingredients and blend until just mixed. Two-thirds fill the muffin tins and place a half date on top of each muffin. Bake for 15–20 min.

Date and orange muffins

Be sure to pit any dates you use. It would be a most unwelcome shock to crunch down on a pit when you least expected it!

1	egg
2 T	melted margarine or butter
½ c	orange juice
1 T	grated orange rind
2 c	chopped dates
⅔ c	sugar
2 t	baking powder
2 c	flour

Lightly oil a muffin tin and preheat the oven to 190 °C. This recipe makes 24 muffins.

Put the first six ingredients into a bowl and mix well. Add the remaining ingredients and blend until just mixed. Two-thirds fill the muffin tins and bake for 15–20 min.

Fruit mince muffins

Either make your own fruit mince or buy some ready made from the grocery store.

2	eggs
375 g	fruit mince
1 c	yoghurt
½ c	melted butter or margarine
1 T	brandy
½ c	sugar
1 t	ground cardamom
2½ c	flour
5 t	baking powder

Lightly oil a muffin tin and preheat the oven to 190 °C. This recipe makes 12 muffins.

Put the first six ingredients into a bowl and mix well. Add the remaining ingredients and blend until just mixed. Bake for 15–20 min.

Garlic muffins

If you like garlic, these are the muffins for you. They go well with soups and salads or can be used in place of garlic bread.

1 c	milk
1	egg
3 T	melted margarine
2-3	cloves garlic, crushed
2 T	chopped chives
1 T	sugar
4 t	baking powder
2 c	flour

Lightly oil a muffin tin and preheat the oven to 190 °C. This recipe makes 12 muffins.

Put the first six ingredients into a bowl and mix well. Add the remaining ingredients and blend until just mixed. Two-thirds fill the muffin tins and bake for 15–20 min.

Gingerbread muffins

These are best made with freshly grated real ginger, if you can be bothered.

1	egg
½ c	golden syrup
½ c	sugar
¼ c	oil
2 t	ginger, ground (or preferably freshly grated)
⅛ t	dry mustard
½ c	yoghurt
¼ t	cinnamon
1 c	flour
1 t	baking powder

Lightly oil a muffin tin and preheat the oven to 180 °C. This recipe makes 12 muffins.
Put the first eight ingredients into a bowl and mix well. Add the remaining ingredients and blend until just mixed. Two-thirds fill the muffin tins and bake for 15–20 min.

Hazelnut muffins

Softly crunchy and absolutely delicious.

2	eggs
¾ c	yoghurt
½ c	melted butter or margarine
½ c	frangelico liqueur
½ c	sugar
1½ c	flour
½ c	chopped hazelnuts
3 t	baking powder

Lightly oil a muffin tin and preheat the oven to 200 °C. This recipe makes 12 muffins.
Put the first five ingredients into a bowl and mix well. Add the remaining ingredients and blend until just mixed. Two-thirds fill the muffin tins and bake for 15–20 min.

Herb muffins

A really delicious muffin, best served with butter and cold sliced meats.

1 T	sugar
1	clove garlic, crushed
½ c	chopped basil
½ c	chopped parsley
1	egg
2 T	oil
1¼ c	sour milk (see page 5)
1½ c	flour
2 t	baking powder
	grated cheese

Lightly oil a muffin tin and preheat the oven to 200 °C. This recipe makes 12 muffins.

Put the first seven ingredients into a bowl and mix well. Add the remaining ingredients except the grated cheese and blend until just mixed. Two-thirds fill the muffin tins. Sprinkle a little cheese on top of each muffin and bake for 15–20 min.

Jam muffins

Instead of strawberry jam you can use whichever other jam you like, or happen to have in the cupboard, for this recipe.

¼ c	melted butter or margarine
1 c	yoghurt
1 c	strawberry jam
1	egg
1 t	grated lemon rind
½ c	sugar
2 t	baking powder
1½ c	flour

Lightly oil a muffin tin and preheat the oven to 200 °C. This recipe makes 12 muffins.

Put the first six ingredients into a bowl and mix well. Add the remaining ingredients and blend until just mixed. Two-thirds fill the muffin tins and bake for 15–20 min.

Kumara muffins

You may think these would be savoury muffins but in fact they're sweet and tasty, with a hint of spice.

½ c	mashed, cooked kumara
⅔ c	milk
3 T	melted margarine or butter
2 T	golden syrup
2	eggs
¼ c	brown sugar
1 t	grated fresh ginger
1 T	baking powder
1½ c	flour

Lightly oil a muffin tin and preheat the oven to 200 °C. This recipe makes 12 muffins.
Put the first seven ingredients into a bowl and mix well. Add the remaining ingredients and blend until just mixed. Two-thirds fill the muffin tins and bake for 20–25 min.

Lemon-cheese and raisin muffins

Moist and tasty muffins to accompany tea or coffee.

⅔ c	milk
	juice and grated rind of 1 lemon
2	eggs
¼ c	white sugar
¼ c	brown sugar
¼ c	lemon cheese
½ c	raisins
1 c	shredded coconut
2 c	flour
1 T	baking powder

Lightly oil a muffin tin and preheat the oven to 190 °C. This recipe makes 14 muffins.
Put the first eight ingredients into a bowl and mix well. Add the remaining ingredients and blend until just mixed. Two-thirds fill the muffin tins and bake for 20–25 min.

Loganberry muffins

For these fruit muffins try to get firm but ripe fresh berries. (The tinned ones are rather soft and tend to break up during the mixing.)

½ c	sugar
1 c	yoghurt
1	egg
2 T	melted butter or margarine
2 c	flour
3 t	baking powder
1 c	loganberries

Lightly oil a muffin tin and preheat the oven to 210 °C. This recipe makes 12 muffins.

Put the first four ingredients into a bowl and mix well. Add the remaining ingredients except the berries and blend until just mixed. Fold in the berries carefully, being sure to mix as little as possible. Two-thirds fill the muffin tins and bake for 15–20 min.

Maple pecan muffins

The pecans give this muffin a crunchy texture and the maple syrup adds flavour.

⅓ c	maple syrup
2 T	melted butter
1	egg
⅔ c	water
1 t	vanilla
½ c	chopped pecans
1½ t	baking powder
1½ c	whole-wheat flour

Lightly oil a muffin tin and preheat the oven to 190 °C. This recipe makes 12 muffins.

Put the first six ingredients into a bowl and mix well. Add the remaining ingredients and blend until just mixed. Two-thirds fill the muffin tins and bake for 15–20 min.

Maple syrup muffins

Plain but with a hint of maple.

½ c	yoghurt
½ c	maple syrup
½ c	melted butter or margarine
1	egg
4 t	baking powder
2 c	flour

Lightly oil a muffin tin and preheat the oven to 200 °C. This recipe makes 12 muffins.

Put the first four ingredients into a bowl and mix well. Add the remaining ingredients and blend until just mixed. Two-thirds fill the muffin tins and bake for 15–20 min.

Marmalade muffins

These are ever so good with tea.

3 T	melted butter
1 c	milk
1	egg
2 t	grated orange rind
½ t	salt
¼ c	sugar
1 T	baking powder
2 c	flour
⅓ c	marmalade

Lightly oil a muffin tin and preheat the oven to 200 °C. This recipe makes 12 muffins.

Put the first six ingredients into a bowl and mix well. Add the remaining ingredients except the marmalade and blend until just mixed. Half fill the muffin tins, then put in a little marmalade and cover with some more batter until the tin is two-thirds full. Bake for 15–20 min.

Onion muffins

These may sound strange, but they are really only savoury muffins ideal for accompanying a meat-based dinner.

1	egg
2 T	oil
1 c	sour milk (see page 5)
¼ c	grated onion
1½ c	flour
2 t	sugar
2 t	baking powder
½ t	dill
1	egg yolk (for glazing)

Lightly oil a muffin tin and preheat the oven to 200 °C. This recipe makes 12 muffins.

Put the first four ingredients into a bowl and mix well, then add the next four ingredients and blend until just mixed. Two-thirds fill the muffin tins, brush each muffin with the egg yolk and bake for 15 min.

Orange muffins

Bitter-sweet orange marmalade provides the fresh orange flavour in these muffins. They remind me of my childhood in California where I used to play in the orange groves. We kids used to pick and eat sweet juicy oranges whenever we were hungry. I wonder what the farmer thought of us, innocently stealing his juicy fruits?

½ c	orange juice
½ c	orange marmalade
¼ c	margarine
1	egg
2 c	flour
¼ c	sugar
3 t	baking powder

Topping

2 T	butter or margarine
¼ c	sugar
3 T	flour
1 t	cinnamon

Lightly oil a muffin tin and preheat the oven to 190 °C. This recipe makes 20 muffins.

Opposite: Fresh and tasty bran muffins (p.19) straight from the oven.

Put the first four ingredients into a bowl and mix well, then add the remaining ingredients and blend until just mixed. Two-thirds fill the muffin tins. Mix together the topping ingredients, sprinkle over each muffin and bake for 20–25 min.

Peach muffins

Sprinkle a little brown sugar on top before baking, to add extra crunch to these sweet and peachy muffins.

1 c	skinned and chopped peaches
½ t	cinnamon
½ c	sugar
1	egg
1 c	yoghurt
⅓ c	butter or margarine, melted
2 T	sherry
2 c	flour
2½ t	baking powder

Lightly oil a muffin tin and preheat the oven to 200 °C. This recipe makes 12 muffins.
Put the first seven ingredients into a bowl and mix well, then add the remaining ingredients and blend until just mixed. Two-thirds fill the muffin tins and bake for 15–20 min.

Peach crumble muffins

The pecans in this really make the difference.

425 g	tin of peaches, chopped
⅓ c	sugar
½ c	chopped pecans
1	egg
1 c	yoghurt
2 T	butter
1 t	cinnamon
1½ c	flour
2 t	baking powder

Opposite: Scones (p. 65) and pikelets (p. 69) with the traditional strawberry jam and whipped cream.

Topping

3 T	flour
2 T	brown sugar
½ t	cinnamon
1 T	butter

Lightly oil a muffin tin and preheat the oven to 200 °C. This recipe makes 12 muffins.

Mix the topping ingredients together, form into a ball and refrigerate until required.

Put the first six ingredients into a bowl and mix well, then add the remaining ingredients and blend until just mixed. Two-thirds fill the muffin tins and grate the topping mixture over each. Bake for 15–20 min.

Peanut muffins

In this recipe the rich flavour from the peanut butter and the subtle crunch from the nuts combine to make a delectable muffin.

1	egg
1 c	milk or yoghurt
1 t	vanilla
¼ c	peanut butter
2 T	melted butter
1 c	salted peanuts
½ c	brown sugar
2 c	flour
4 t	baking powder

Lightly oil a muffin tin and preheat the oven to 190 °C. This recipe makes 12 muffins.

Put the first six ingredients into a bowl and mix well, then add the remaining ingredients and blend until just mixed. Two-thirds fill the muffin tins and bake for 20–25 min.

Peanut butter muffins

These are for those people who like the taste of peanut butter but not the crunch of the nuts. (My kids don't particularly like muffins with nuts in them and so this recipe has been a good alternative.)

1 c	yoghurt
1	egg
⅓ c	margarine, melted
¼ c	peanut butter
⅓ c	sugar
2 c	flour
3 t	baking powder

Lightly oil a muffin tin and preheat the oven to 200 °C. This recipe makes 12 muffins.

Put the first five ingredients into a bowl and mix well, then add the remaining ingredients and blend until just mixed. Two-thirds fill the muffin tins and bake for 15 min.

Peanut butter and jam muffins

These take me back to my schooldays when lunch was a peanut butter and jelly (jam) sandwich. These flavours must be almost as American as apple pie.

1 T	melted margarine
½ c	peanut butter
1	egg
1 c	sour milk (see page 5)
2 T	sugar
2 c	flour
1 T	baking powder

Topping

3 T	crushed salted peanuts
4 T	sugar
2 T	butter
	strawberry jam for the middle

Lightly oil a muffin tin and preheat the oven to 200 °C. This recipe makes 12 muffins.

Put the first five ingredients into a bowl and mix well, then add the flour and baking powder and blend until just mixed. Put a large spoonful of the batter into each muffin tin, then drop a small spoonful of jam in the centre of each and cover with remaining batter. Sprinkle with the topping mixture and bake for 10–15 min.

Pineapple muffins

Juicy chunks of pineapple keep these muffins lovely and moist.

½ c	chopped pineapple
1 c	pineapple juice
1	egg
2 T	melted margarine
¼ c	sugar
2 c	flour
4 t	baking powder

Lightly oil a muffin tin and preheat the oven to 200 °C. This recipe makes 12 muffins.

Put the first five ingredients into a bowl and mix well, then add the remaining ingredients and blend until just mixed. Two-thirds fill the muffin tins and bake for 15 min.

Poppy seed muffins

These have a delightful crunchy texture, but watch out for poppy seeds stuck in your teeth when you smile.

1½ c	yoghurt
¼ c	oil
2 t	vanilla
⅓ c	sugar
¼ c	poppy seeds
2	eggs
1¾ c	flour
2 t	baking powder

Lightly oil a muffin tin and preheat the oven to 190 °C. This recipe makes 12 muffins.

Put the first six ingredients into a bowl and mix well, then add the remaining ingredients and blend until just mixed. Two-thirds fill the muffin tins and bake for 10–15 min.

Potato muffins

A savoury muffin to go with soup or to accompany a meal of roast pork — really rather different.

2	eggs
1 c	yoghurt
⅓ c	melted butter or margarine
1½ c	grated raw potato
2 T	grated onion
1 T	sugar
1 t	caraway seeds
2 c	flour
4 t	baking powder

Lightly oil a muffin tin and preheat the oven to 190 °C. This recipe makes 12 muffins.

Put the first seven ingredients into a bowl and mix well, then add the remaining ingredients and blend until just mixed. Two-thirds fill the muffin tins and bake for 20–25 min.

Dilly potato muffins

Another savoury muffin but with fresh dill to liven up the taste buds.

½ c	yoghurt
⅔ c	mashed potatoes
¾ c	sour milk (see page 5)
¼ c	melted butter
2	eggs
3 T	chopped dill
2 c	flour
2 t	baking powder

Lightly oil a muffin tin and preheat the oven to 200 °C. This recipe makes 12 muffins.

Put the first six ingredients into a bowl and mix well, then add the remaining ingredients and blend until just mixed. Two-thirds fill the muffin tins and bake for 15–20 min.

Prune muffins

These are really scrumptious, and they keep you regular too!

1	egg
2 T	melted butter or margarine
1 c	yoghurt
½ t	allspice
2 t	baking powder
⅓ c	sugar
1½ c	flour

For the middle
½ c	prune purée
1 T	melted butter
1 T	sugar
½ t	cinnamon
¼ c	chopped walnuts

Topping
1 t	cinnamon
3 T	sugar

Lightly oil a muffin tin and preheat the oven to 200 °C. This recipe makes 12 muffins.

Put the first four ingredients into a bowl and mix well, then add the baking powder, sugar and flour and blend until just mixed. In a separate bowl mix the ingredients for the filling. Put a large spoonful of batter into each muffin tin, drop a small spoonful of the filling in the centre of each and top with the remaining batter. Sprinkle with the cinnamon and sugar and bake for 10–15 min.

Pumpkin muffins

If you have any leftover mashed pumpkin from making pumpkin pies, this is a great way to use it up.

¾ c	yoghurt
½ c	mashed pumpkin
3 T	oil
1	egg
½ c	brown sugar
⅛ t	cloves
1 t	cinnamon
2 c	flour
1 T	baking powder

Lightly oil a muffin tin and preheat the oven to 200 °C. This recipe makes 12 muffins.

Put the first seven ingredients into a bowl and mix well, then add the remaining ingredients and blend until just mixed. Two-thirds fill the muffin tins and bake for 15–20 min.

Pumpkin bran muffins

1 c	mashed pumpkin
½ c	melted butter
⅔ c	yoghurt
2	eggs
1¾ c	bran
1 c	chopped pecans
½ c	raisins (optional)
2 t	mixed spice
3 t	baking powder
⅔ c	sugar
2 c	flour

Lightly oil a muffin tin and preheat the oven to 190 °C. This recipe makes 20 muffins.

Put the first eight ingredients into a bowl and mix well, then add the remaining ingredients and blend until just mixed. Two-thirds fill the muffin tins and bake for 10–15 min.

Pumpkin pecan muffins

¾ c	brown sugar
¼ c	golden syrup
1 c	yoghurt
2 c	mashed pumpkin
2	eggs
1 c	chopped pecans
1 t	grated fresh ginger
2 t	cinnamon
1¼ T	baking powder
2¾ c	flour

Lightly oil a muffin tin and preheat the oven to 190 °C. This recipe makes 20 muffins.

Put the first eight ingredients into a bowl and mix well, then add the remaining ingredients and blend until just mixed. Two-thirds fill the muffin tins and bake for 15–20 min.

Pumpkin seed muffins

Either make your own roasted pumpkin seeds and shell them, or buy them already processed from health food stores. Sunflower seeds are an OK substitute.

1	egg
⅓ c	oil
½ c	mashed pumpkin
¾ c	yoghurt
1 t	cinnamon
¼ c	shelled, chopped and toasted pumpkin seeds
½ c	sugar
1 T	baking powder
1¾ c	flour

Lightly oil a muffin tin and preheat the oven to 200 °C. This recipe makes 12 muffins.
Put the first seven ingredients into a bowl and mix well, then add the remaining ingredients and blend until just mixed. Two-thirds fill the muffin tins and bake for 15–20 min.

Raisin muffins

Plump, juicy raisins and sweet fresh almonds go together well in this muffin.

¾ c	yoghurt
2	eggs
½ c	melted butter or margarine
1 t	vanilla
½ c	raisins
½ c	slivered almonds
1 T	grated orange rind
1 t	cinnamon
½ c	sugar
2 c	flour
2 t	baking powder

Lightly oil a muffin tin and preheat the oven to 190 °C. This recipe makes 15 muffins.
Put the first nine ingredients into a bowl and mix well, then add the remaining ingredients and blend until just mixed. Two-thirds fill the muffin tins and bake for 20–25 min.

Rum and raisin muffins

1 c	raisins, soaked in ½ c rum and drained
1	egg
⅓ c	melted butter or margarine
1 t	vanilla
1 c	yoghurt
½ c	sugar
2 c	flour
2 t	baking powder

Lightly oil a muffin tin and preheat the oven to 190 °C. This recipe makes 12 muffins.
Put the first six ingredients into a bowl and mix well, then add the remaining ingredients and blend until just mixed. You may like to add a little of the rum in which the raisins were soaking if the batter is a little dry. Two-thirds fill the muffin tins and bake for 15–20 min.

Spicy raisin muffins

All the flavour of the Spice Islands in one delicious muffin.

2 T	melted butter or margarine
1 c	sour milk (see page 5)
2	eggs
1¼ c	raisins
½ t	allspice
1 t	cinnamon
2 t	baking powder
½ c	sugar
1½ c	flour

Lightly oil a muffin tin and preheat the oven to 200 °C. This recipe makes 12 muffins.
Put the first six ingredients into a bowl and mix well, then add the remaining ingredients and blend until just mixed. Two-thirds fill the muffin tins and bake for 15–20 min.

Rice muffins

Brown, white or red rice — whichever type you use, these are still nice muffins.

1 c	yoghurt
2 T	melted butter
1	egg
1 c	cooked rice
1 t	cinnamon
1 t	nutmeg
2 t	baking powder
¼ c	sugar
1¼ c	flour

Lightly oil a muffin tin and preheat the oven to 200 °C. This recipe makes 12 muffins.

Put the first six ingredients into a bowl and mix well, then add the remaining ingredients and blend until just mixed. Two-thirds fill the muffin tins and bake for 15 min.

Savoury rice muffins

These are great with a meal — any meal!

2	eggs
1½ c	sour milk (see page 5)
6 T	melted butter
1 c	cooked brown rice
½ t	thyme
1 t	sage
1 t	grated onion
5 t	baking powder
1 T	sugar
2 c	flour

Lightly oil a muffin tin and preheat the oven to 190 °C. This recipe makes 12 muffins.

Put the first seven ingredients into a bowl and mix well, then add the remaining ingredients and blend until just mixed. Two-thirds fill the muffin tins and bake for 15–20 min.

Tropical rice muffins

½ c	cooked brown rice
2	eggs
⅔ c	yoghurt
¼ c	oil
⅓ c	sugar
½ c	shredded coconut
1 T	baking powder
1 t	cinnamon
1½ c	flour
½ c	chopped pineapple

Lightly oil a muffin tin and preheat the oven to 190 °C. This recipe makes 12 muffins.

Put the first six ingredients into a bowl and mix well, then add the remaining ingredients, except the pineapple, and blend until just mixed. Two-thirds fill the muffin tins, sprinkle a little chopped pineapple on top of each muffin and bake for 15–20 min.

Salami and herb muffins

These are almost a meal in themselves. You can get sun-dried tomatoes in your local deli or make your own and store them in oil until you use them.

2	eggs
1	clove garlic, crushed
⅓ c	chopped green stuffed olives
¼ c	chopped salami
¼ c	chopped dried tomatoes
½ t	oregano
½ c	oil
⅔ c	sour milk (see page 5)
½ c	chopped spring onions
1 T	sugar
2 c	flour
3 t	baking powder
	grated cheese

Lightly oil a muffin tin and preheat the oven to 200 °C. This recipe makes 12 muffins.

Put the first 10 ingredients into a bowl and mix well, then add the remaining ingredients and blend until just mixed. Two-thirds fill the muffin tins and sprinkle each with a little grated cheese. Bake for 15–20 min.

Sesame seed muffins

It's the sesame oil that gives these muffins a distinctly Middle-eastern flavour. Make sure that the oil is fresh.

⅓ c	toasted sesame seeds
1	egg
¼ c	yoghurt
1 c	milk
⅓ c	melted butter or margarine
1 T	sesame oil
⅓ c	brown sugar
2 t	baking powder
1½ c	flour

Lightly oil a muffin tin and preheat the oven to 200 °C. This recipe makes 12 muffins.

Put the first seven ingredients into a bowl and mix well, then add the remaining ingredients and blend until just mixed. Two-thirds fill the muffin tins and sprinkle a few sesame seeds on top of each muffin. Bake for 15–20 min.

Sherry muffins

A friend in Madrid sent me this recipe. I think it is representative of Spain, the country of strong coffee and good sherry ... and lots of other wonderful things too!

2	eggs
⅓ c	coffee
⅓ c	sherry
4 T	melted butter or margarine
1 t	vanilla
⅔ c	brown sugar
2 c	flour
½ c	bran
2 t	baking powder
½ c	chopped nuts

Lightly oil a muffin tin and preheat the oven to 190 °C. This recipe makes 12 muffins.

Put the first six ingredients into a bowl and mix well, then add the remaining ingredients and blend until just mixed. Two-thirds fill the muffin tins and bake for 10–15 min.

Soy sausage muffins

These are for the vegetable animal in us all.

1 c	sour milk (see page 5)
3 T	melted butter or margarine
2	eggs
1 T	sherry
1 c	peeled and chopped apple
⅓ c	grated onion
½ c	grated raw potato
½ t	celery seed
¼ t	allspice
¼ t	pepper
1 T	brown sugar
1 c	chopped soy sausage
1 T	baking powder
1¾ c	wholemeal flour

Lightly oil a muffin tin and preheat the oven to 190 °C. This recipe makes 15 muffins.
Put the first 12 ingredients into a bowl and mix well, then add the remaining ingredients and blend until just mixed. Two-thirds fill the muffin tins and bake for 15–20 min.

Spice muffins

'Sugar and spice and all things nice', that's what these muffins are made of.

½ c	yoghurt
¼ c	milk
⅓ c	golden syrup
¼ c	melted butter or margarine
1	egg
½ t	grated ginger
¼ t	nutmeg
½ t	allspice
1 t	cinnamon
½ c	sugar
1½ c	flour
2 t	baking powder

Lightly oil a muffin tin and preheat the oven to 200 °C. This recipe makes 12 muffins.

Put the first 10 ingredients into a bowl and mix well, then add the remaining ingredients and blend until just mixed. Two-thirds fill the muffin tins and bake for 15–20 min.

Strawberry jam muffins

Sweet strawberry surprises in the centre are the key to these muffins.

⅓ c	melted butter or margarine
1 c	yoghurt
2	eggs
½ c	sugar
2 t	baking powder
⅔ c	oat bran
1¼ c	flour
¼ c	sliced almonds
½ c	strawberry jam

Lightly oil a muffin tin and preheat the oven to 200 °C. This recipe makes 12 muffins.

Put the first four ingredients into a bowl and mix well, then add the remaining ingredients except the jam and blend until just mixed. Place a spoonful of the batter into each muffin tin, then put a little strawberry jam into the centre of each muffin and top off with the remaining batter. Scatter a few extra sliced almonds on top and bake for 15–20 min.

Sugar-free muffins

This recipe was created by Paul Scott because he just couldn't find a truly healthy no-nonsense muffin to complement his health-conscious lifestyle. Thanks, Paul; no muffin book is complete without such a recipe.

2	eggs
1 c	soy milk
3 T	oil
1 c	grated carrot
1 c	raisins
2 T	sesame seeds
3 T	sunflower seeds
1 t	mixed spice
1½ c	coconut
1 c	wholemeal flour
1 c	rye flour
3 t	baking powder

Lightly oil a muffin tin and preheat the oven to 190 °C. This recipe makes 15 muffins.

Put the first nine ingredients into a bowl and mix well. Add the remaining ingredients and blend until just mixed. Two-thirds fill the muffin tins and bake for 15–20 min.

Tramper's muffins

Rustle up a batch of these before you set out for a day's tramping and you won't have to meet up with the growly-tummy monster on the track.

¼ c	oil
1 c	yoghurt
1	egg
¼ c	shredded coconut
¼ c	chopped nuts
¼ c	raisins
¼ c	chopped dried apricots
¼ c	chocolate chips
¼ c	sugar
1 c	bran
1¼ c	flour
1½ t	baking powder

Lightly oil a muffin tin and preheat the oven to 200 °C. This recipe makes 12 muffins.

Put the first 10 ingredients into a bowl and mix well, then add the remaining ingredients and blend until just mixed. Two-thirds fill a muffin tin and bake for 15–20 min.

Walnut muffins

It is nice to go out nutting, where you can, and gather your own walnuts for this recipe. Of course, store-bought walnuts will do just as well, but they aren't as much fun.

1 c	yoghurt
¼ c	melted butter or margarine
1 t	vanilla
1	egg
½ c	brown sugar
1 c	chopped walnuts
1 T	baking powder
1¾ c	flour

Lightly oil a muffin tin and preheat the oven to 190 °C. This recipe makes 12 muffins.

Put the first six ingredients into a bowl and mix well, then add the remaining ingredients and blend until just mixed. Two-thirds fill the muffin tins and bake for 15–20 min.

Walnut and honey muffins

The Greeks had a great idea when they combined honey and walnuts in their baclava. These muffins modestly attempt to imitate this.

1	egg
3 T	melted butter or margarine
1 c	yoghurt
½ c	sugar
2½ t	baking powder
1½ c	flour

Filling

⅔ c	brown sugar
1 c	chopped walnuts
1½ t	cinnamon
3 T	melted butter

Topping

¾ c	honey

Lightly oil a muffin tin and preheat the oven to 200 °C. This recipe makes 12 muffins.

Put the first four ingredients into a bowl and mix well, then add the baking powder and flour and blend until just mixed. In a separate bowl mix all the ingredients for the filling. Put a large spoonful of the batter into each muffin tin, then a small spoonful of the filling and then another spoonful of the batter. Bake for 15–20 min then spread honey on the top.

Opposite: Perfect with coffee, waffles (p. 72) can come in many different shapes.

Scones

Hints for successful scone-making

Rule number one when making scones is to mix them as little as possible. After that everything is a matter of personal preference. You can roll the dough out and cut it into shapes or you can drop it from the spoon and have rougher-shaped scones. You can place them close together on the baking tray or separate them into individual scones. Scones can be glazed or left floury. A basic scone recipe can be turned into almost anything, from a sweet currant scone to a savoury cheese one.

The generally accepted method of mixing scones is by cutting or rubbing the butter into the flour. First ensure that your milk is quite cold and that the butter is at room temperature, then rub the butter into the flour mixture until it is the consistency of coarse meal. Add the milk and blend until just mixed. Knead if required, but only briefly, then shape the scones and bake.

Scones can be reheated, but in my opinion are best fresh from the oven.

Scone recipes

Basic scone recipe

My friend Linda points out that the mixing method I use is a two-bowl method and so makes more of a mess than just rubbing in the butter by hand. She is right, but I don't have the patience to rub all the butter into the flour properly. I know that the food-processor method will give me a better flour-butter mix and so a better end result. It's a matter of knowing which method works best for you.

2 c	flour
½ t	salt
3 t	baking powder
⅓ c	butter
⅔ c	milk

Preheat the oven to 230 °C. This recipe makes 18 scones.
Put the first four ingredients into a food processor and whizz until they are the consistency of oat bran. Transfer this mixture into another bowl and add the milk, blending until just mixed. Turn out the dough on to a floured counter and knead lightly or just pat together. (The less you handle the dough, the lighter the scones will be.) Cut into shapes or slice into squares and place on an ungreased baking sheet. Bake for 12–15 min.

Opposite: What could be nicer for afternoon tea? Muffins are easy to make, versatile and taste great. *By courtesy of Miracle Margarine*

Buttermilk scones

The original recipe suggested that you cut these out into the shape of rabbits and have them for Easter breakfast. That's quite a nice idea, and because they are so quick to make, they don't interfere with hunting for Easter eggs.

⅓ c	sugar
3 c	flour
1 T	baking powder
¾ c	butter
¾ c	mixed currants, chopped dates and citron
1 c	buttermilk or sour milk (see page 5)

Preheat the oven to 220 °C.
Put the first four ingredients into a food processor and whizz to the consistency of oat bran. Transfer this mixture into another bowl and add the fruit and milk, blending until it is just mixed. Turn out the dough on to a floured counter and knead lightly. Roll or pat out and cut into shapes. Put onto ungreased non-stick baking sheets, sprinkle with a little sugar and cinnamon and bake for 12–15 min.

Basic cheese scone

Get the kids to 'help' you make these. They can't go too far wrong and they will enjoy the making and the eating.

2 c	flour
2 t	baking powder
1 T	oil
1 c	milk
75 g	grated cheese
¼ t	salt

Preheat the oven to 220 °C.
Put all the ingredients into a bowl and lightly mix, then turn the dough out onto a floured counter and knead lightly. You may need a little extra flour. Pat into a rectangle and cut into squares. Put the dough onto a non-stick baking sheet and bake for 10–15 min.

Ruth's 'hands-off' cheese scones

Now you can even make scones without getting bits of the dough caught in your diamond rings or around your fingernails. Pretty clever, don't you think? These are made in a muffin tin rather than on a baking sheet.

200 g	flour
2 t	baking powder
25 g	cold butter
50 g	cheese
1 c	milk

Preheat the oven to 230 °C.

Lightly oil a muffin tin. Put the flour and baking powder into a bowl. Put the bowl onto a kitchen scales and grate in the butter and cheese straight from the block until you have the right weight of each. Toss this lot together and add the milk. Lightly mix, then spoon mixture into the muffin tins. Bake for 15–20 min.

Wholemeal scones

This is another basic recipe which you can make more interesting by putting in raisins, nuts, seeds or whatever you like.

1 c	wholemeal flour
1 c	flour
2 t	baking powder
½ t	salt
30 g	butter
1 c	milk or a little less

Preheat the oven to 230 °C.

Put the first five ingredients into a food processor and whizz to the consistency of oat bran. Add the milk and blend until just mixed. Turn out dough onto a floured counter and knead lightly. Pat into a rectangle and cut into shapes. Put the scones onto a baking sheet and bake for 10–15 min.

Pumpkin scones

1 T	butter
½ c	sugar
2¼ c	flour
2½ t	baking powder
1 c	mashed pumpkin
1	egg

Preheat the oven to 220 °C.

Put the first four ingredients into a food processor and whizz to the consistency of oat bran. Transfer to another bowl and stir in the egg and pumpkin until just mixed. Turn out the dough onto a lightly floured counter and knead briefly. Put the mixture onto the baking sheet, pat into a circle and cut into triangles but do not separate. Sprinkle with brown sugar and bake for 15–20 min.

Cinnamon currant scones

2 c	flour
1 t	baking powder
1 t	cream of tartar
1 t	cinnamon
4 T	butter
1 c	sour milk (see page 5)
1 c	currants

Preheat the oven to 230 °C.
Put the first five ingredients into a food processor and whizz to the consistency of oat bran. Transfer to another bowl, add the milk and currants and mix until just blended. Turn out the dough onto a floured counter and pat into a rectangle. Cut into squares. Place on a non-stick baking sheet and bake for 10–15 min.

Butterscotch scones

This is more like a scone roll. It is scone dough rolled with a filling and sliced so your scone is a swirled pattern. It's quick and delicious.

Filling

| ⅓ c | butter |
| ¾ c | brown sugar |

2 c	flour
1½ T	baking powder
2 T	butter
⅔ c	milk

Preheat the oven to 190 °C.
Cream the butter and brown sugar together for the filling and set aside.
Put the flour, baking powder and butter into a food processor and whizz to the consistency of oat bran. Transfer to another bowl, add the milk and mix until just blended. Turn out onto a floured counter, knead lightly, pat into an oblong and spread with the filling. Roll up and slice into 2-cm slices. Place the slices on a tray and bake for 15–20 min.

Variations
Fill with any of the following:
- chocolate chips
- Nutella
- honey, chopped walnuts and cinnamon
- butter and orange marmalade.

Pikelets

I've always thought of pikelets as small, thick but light pancakes. They are often served cold with butter and jam but are very nice served warm while fresh from the pan. You can add fruit to the batter to jazz it up, but it is not necessary. Pikelets spread with hundreds and thousands are good for kids' parties. For picnics, spread with butter; with tea and coffee, serve with butter and jam. Pikelets are fast to make and can be cooked well ahead of time.

Hints for pikelet-making

- Be sure to have the pan fairly hot and lightly oiled or buttered.
- A heavy-bottomed pan is best for frying at high temperatures.
- Spoon the batter into the hot pan and when it bubbles on the top, turn it once.

Pikelet recipes

Basic pikelet recipe

Pikelets by any other name are pancakes and definitely not crepes. A pikelet should be thick but light and about the size of a large Agee jar lid. They are great made ahead of time.

½ c	milk
1½ T	butter
1 c	flour
1 t	baking powder
2 T	sugar
1	egg

Melt the butter in the milk and set aside. Put all the ingredients into a food processor and whizz until the batter is a smooth consistency. (This can also be done in a bowl by hand.)
Lightly oil a heavy-bottomed pan and make sure it is hot before you pour large spoonfuls of the batter onto it.
Turn the pikelet when it is bubbly and cook until the other side is golden. Remove to a cooling rack. Serve with lashings of butter and a touch of jam.

Breakfast pikelets

This is just the American version of pikelets. Try throwing in a handful of toasted sesame seeds for a different and tasty version.

1 c	flour
3½ t	baking powder
⅓ c	full-cream milk powder
1 c	milk
2 T	sugar
1	egg
2 T	butter

Melt the butter in the milk over a gentle heat, or in the microwave. Put all the ingredients into a food processor and whizz until the batter is a smooth consistency.

Lightly oil and heat a heavy-bottomed pan and drop spoonfuls of the batter onto it. When the pikelet is bubbly, turn it and continue cooking until the bottom is golden. Remove to a cooling rack.

Shazz's pikelets

Or 'what every schoolgirl and schoolboy should know how to make'. These pikelets are easy, tasty and always work.

6 T	flour
3 t	baking powder
1	egg
1 T	melted butter
	milk

Put the flour, baking powder, egg and melted butter into a bowl and add enough milk to make a smooth batter. Heat a lightly oiled pan and drop spoonfuls of the batter onto it. Turn pikelets when they are bubbly and cook until the bottom is golden.

Rhona's pikelets

1 c	flour
½ t	cream of tartar
1 t	baking soda
1 T	sugar
1	egg
1 T	golden syrup
½ c	milk

Put the first three ingredients into a bowl, add the sugar, egg, syrup and half of the milk and stir until just mixed. Add the remaining milk and beat with a spoon until smooth. Lightly oil a heavy-bottomed pan and heat. Fry until all the bubbles just break on top, then turn and continue cooking until done.

Waffles

Waffles are fun. Waffles are fast. Waffles are delicious with all sorts of sauces and toppings. Kids love waffles as a weekend treat, and so do grown-ups! We often have people around for breakfast on weekends and waffles can make an ideal starter for guests to top with anything from maple syrup to bacon and eggs.

In this section I list several different sorts of waffles and a whole bunch of possible variations for you to try. I've also given a few different sauces and toppings, but the list is only limited by your taste preferences.

Of course to make waffles you will need a waffle iron. There is no way around that, but you will be pleased to know that there are many different types available. All of the batters in this book are suitable for any waffle iron.

Cooking times for waffles vary depending on the waffle iron, but you will quickly learn the best timing for your waffles — usually a minute or two.

Waffle recipes

Basic waffle batter

I use this recipe most often — it makes great waffles. Any leftover waffles, should you be so lucky, can be eaten later, heated up in the microwave or toaster. (Waffles with some of last night's salmon pate or chicken and gravy make a tasty lunch.)

4	eggs
2¼ c	milk
1 t	vanilla essence
⅔ c	oil or melted butter
2 T	sugar
2 T	baking powder
3 c	flour

Put all the ingredients into a food processor and whizz until the batter is smooth and lump-free. You can do this in a mixing bowl by hand too, but take care to mix well so there are no lumps.

Heat your waffle iron and pour in just enough batter so that it doesn't creep over the edge when cooking. (It will take a bit of practice to work out the correct amount of batter for your particular waffle iron.) Cook waffles until golden.

Serve the waffles hot from the iron with dabs of butter and lots of maple syrup, or topped with any of the syrups and sauces listed on page 75.

Variations

Sesame waffles — add ¼ c sesame seeds.
Orange waffles — add the grated rind of 1 or 2 oranges.
Cornmeal waffles — substitute 1 cup of cornmeal for 1 cup of flour.
Wholemeal waffles — substitute 1 cup wholemeal flour for 1 cup of flour.

Basic yeast batter for waffles

These take a little longer to prepare, since the yeast needs time to get started. The thing about these waffles is that they are more substantial, more breadlike. Try them and see what you think.

1 T	dry yeast
1 T	sugar
2 c	warm milk
4	eggs
1 t	vanilla
½ c	melted butter
2½ c	flour

Put the yeast, sugar and warm milk into a plastic bowl and let it stand in a warm place to form a sponge. (A sponge is the foam that is formed when the yeast is being activated.) Once the sponge has formed, which should take about 5–10 min., mix it by hand or in a food processor with all the other ingredients to form a smooth batter. Cover the bowl with a tea towel and let it stand for about 30 min. before use.
Heat your waffle iron, put in as much batter as is right for your iron and cook until the waffle is golden and inviting. Serve glazed with a light mixture of icing sugar and water or your favourite topping.

Rice waffles

A good use for leftover rice. (But if you haven't any leftover rice, don't let that stop you from trying these interesting waffles.)

2	eggs, separated
1½ c	milk
⅓ c	melted butter or margarine
3 t	baking powder
1½ c	flour
½ c	cooked rice

Beat the egg whites till they form soft white peaks. Set aside.
Put the milk, butter, egg yolks, baking powder and flour into a food processor and whizz to a smooth batter. Briefly stir in the rice and fold in the egg whites. Heat your waffle iron, pour in the batter and cook the waffles until golden.

Apple waffles

These are moist and yummy, but you'll have to watch them a little because they have fruit in the batter which sometimes sticks to the irons. Great served with a sprinkling of icing sugar.

1½ c	milk
⅓ c	melted butter or margarine
2	eggs
½ c	applesauce or chopped, peeled apple
1 T	sugar
1 t	grated lemon rind
3 t	baking powder
1½ c	flour

Put all the ingredients into the food processor and whizz to a smooth consistency. Heat the waffle iron, pour in the batter and cook the waffles until golden.

Bran waffles

Make these with wheat or oat bran. Try adding some cracked wheat that has been soaked overnight and squeezed; or add rolled oats when using oat bran.

1½ c	yoghurt
½ c	milk
4	eggs
¾ c	flour
¾ c	bran
2½ t	baking powder

Put all the ingredients into a food processor and whizz to a smooth consistency. Heat your waffle iron, pour in the batter and cook until golden.

Fresh fruit waffles

This is a basic recipe for waffle batter with fruit incorporated. The main thing to remember is to cook such waffles a little longer than you would waffles without fruit. Also, be careful not to let the fruit stick to the iron – you might need to lightly oil the iron. Suggested fruits are blueberries, pineapple, feijoa and strawberry. Serve with whipped cream and fruit or a fruit syrup over the top.

1½ c	milk
⅓ c	melted butter or oil
3	eggs
3 t	baking powder
1½ c	flour
¾ c	fruit

Put all the ingredients except the fruit into the food processor and whizz to a smooth consistency, then fold in the fruit. Heat the waffle iron, pour in the batter and cook the waffles until golden brown.

Sauces for waffles

Of course, these sauces are also good for pikelets, pancakes or anything else that you want to sauce up.

Orange syrup

⅔ c	sugar
⅔ c	water
3 T	butter
⅔ c	orange juice

Boil the sugar and water together for 5 min., then add the remaining ingredients and boil for about a minute longer.

Orange butter sauce

3 T	sugar
	grated rind of 1 orange
3 T	butter
1 T	orange juice
3 T	curacao

Put all the ingredients into a small pot and simmer gently until butter has melted. Stir well and serve over waffles.

Brown sugar syrup

1 c   brown sugar
½ c   water
⅓ c   butter
3 T   rum or brandy (optional)

Put the sugar and water in a small pot and boil for 3 min. Add the butter and beat together until melted. Stir in the rum or brandy.

Honey syrup

This honey syrup is just a little enriched with butter. (Of course, you can use plain honey as it comes from the bee! If you heat it up a little in the microwave or on the stove you'll find it is more runny and easier to spread.)

½ c   honey
¼ c   water
⅓ c   butter

Put all the ingredients into a pot and warm gently. Beat together and serve.

Index for Muffins

Index for Pikelets

Index for Scones

Index for Waffles